Can't wait too meet the new handsome guy. Excited to see how much joy and laughter he's sure to bring to your life!

Auntie can't wait to see and snuggle her nephew!

— Katie ♡

This book belongs to:

_____

MY DOG
IS MY
BEST FRIEND

I LOVE MY DOG

AND MY DOG LOVES ME.

MY DOG TEACHES ME

WHAT A GOOD FRIEND
I CAN BE.

WE LOVE PLAYING CATCH

AND RUNNING ALL AROUND,

AND SEEING HER HAPPY

MAKES ME HAPPY AND PROUD.

WE LOVE GOING ON WALKS

AND EXPLORING THE WILD,

AND COME RAIN

OR COME SHINE,

SHE NEVER LEAVES MY SIDE.

I LOVE TEACHING HER TRICKS

AND GIVING HER TREATS,

AND TOGETHER WE LEARN
SO MANY THINGS.

I LOVE MY DOG

AND MY DOG LOVES ME,

AND MY DOG TEACHES ME

HOW GOOD BEING
A GOOD FRIEND CAN BE.

THE END

what does your best friend mean to you?

_____

_____

_____

_____

_____

Add your favorite photo
of you with your best friend!

Draw a picture of you with your best friend!

Mark yours and your
furry friend's handprints
and paw prints right here!
Friends forever!

ABOUT THE AUTHOR

Jennifer L. Trace has been a graphic designer and teacher before becoming a mother of two. Whenever she teaches kids, she loves inspiring them through free play, story-telling, and imagination. Jennifer enjoys cooking, traveling, and adventure sports during her free time.

CPSIA information can be obtained
at www.ICGtesting.com
Printed in the USA
BVHW061026300921
617775BV00004B/282